APPETIZER

RECIPE BOOK TO WRITE IN

Belongs to

....

....

....

Appetizer Recipe Book to Write In is one of the eight cookbooks published as part of a larger collection designed to help you write your own recipes in one place and have them at hand when you cook your favorite meals.

This **Special Collection** also includes:

- SOUPS
- SALADS
- PASTRIES
- DIET RECIPES
- OVEN RECIPES
- VEGAN RECIPES
- CAKES AND PIES

# Table of Contents

Recipe	Page

Table of Contents

Recipe	Page

Table of Contents

Recipe	Page

Table of Contents

Recipe	Page

Table of Contents

Recipe

Page

Recipe:____ 

Prep time:________   Cook time:________   Servings:________

Ingredients	Directions

Notes

Recipe: ____ 

Prep time: _______ Cook time: _______ Servings: _______

Ingredients

Directions

Notes

Recipe:_______________________________________

Prep time:________   Cook time:________   Servings:________

Ingredients

Directions

Notes

Recipe:____ 

Prep time:_______ **Cook time:**_______ **Servings:**_______

Ingredients | Directions

Notes

Recipe:____ 

Prep time:________   Cook time:________   Servings:________

Ingredients

Directions

Notes

Recipe:____ 

Prep time:_______   Cook time:_______   Servings:_______

Ingredients

Directions

Notes

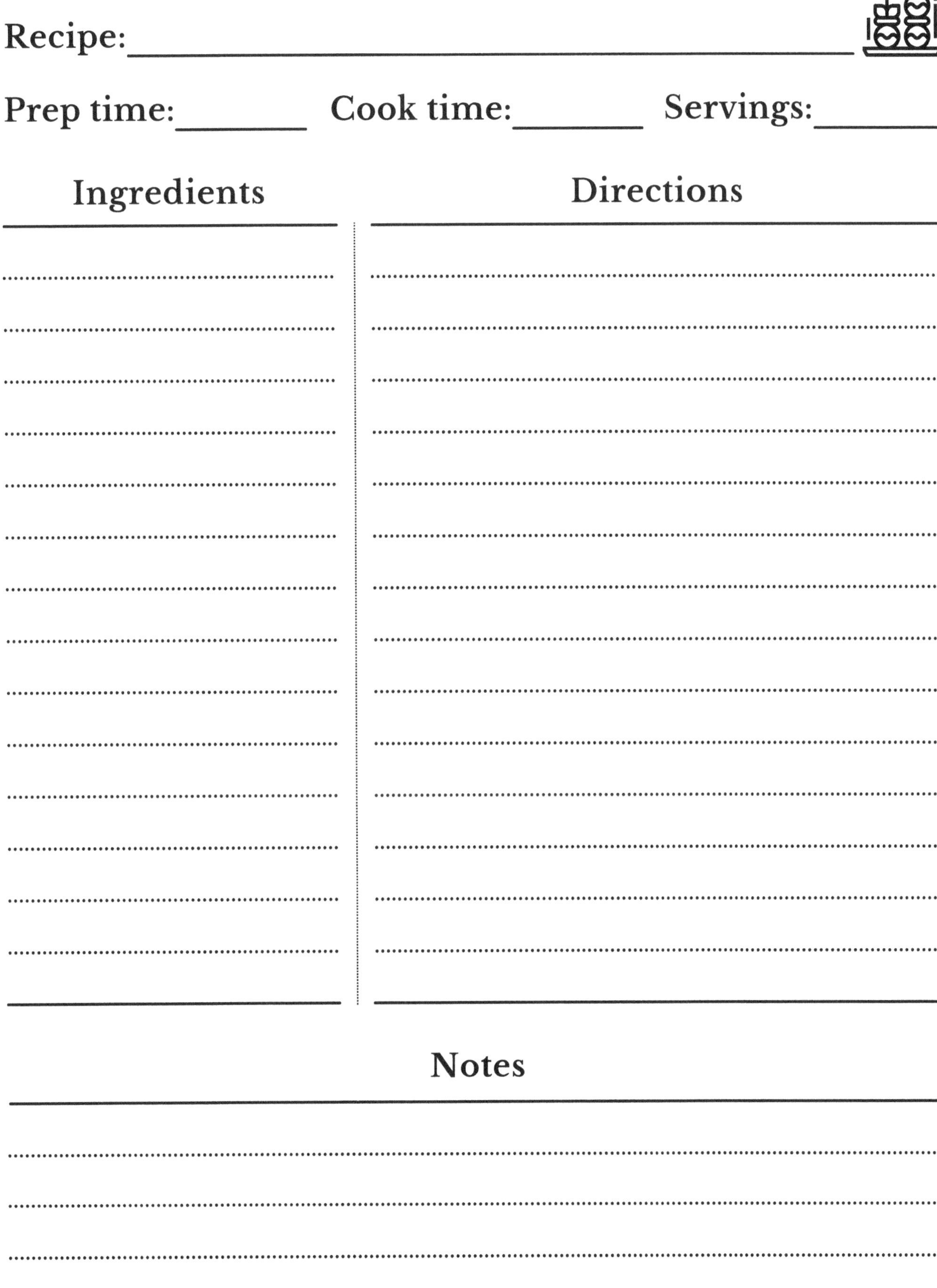

Recipe:____

Prep time:________ Cook time:________ Servings:________

Ingredients

Directions

Notes

Recipe:____ 

Prep time:________   Cook time:________   Servings:________

Ingredients

Directions

Notes

Recipe:____ 

Prep time:_______   Cook time:_______   Servings:_______

Ingredients

Directions

Notes

Recipe: _______________________ 

Prep time: _______ **Cook time:** _______ **Servings:** _______

Ingredients

Directions

Notes

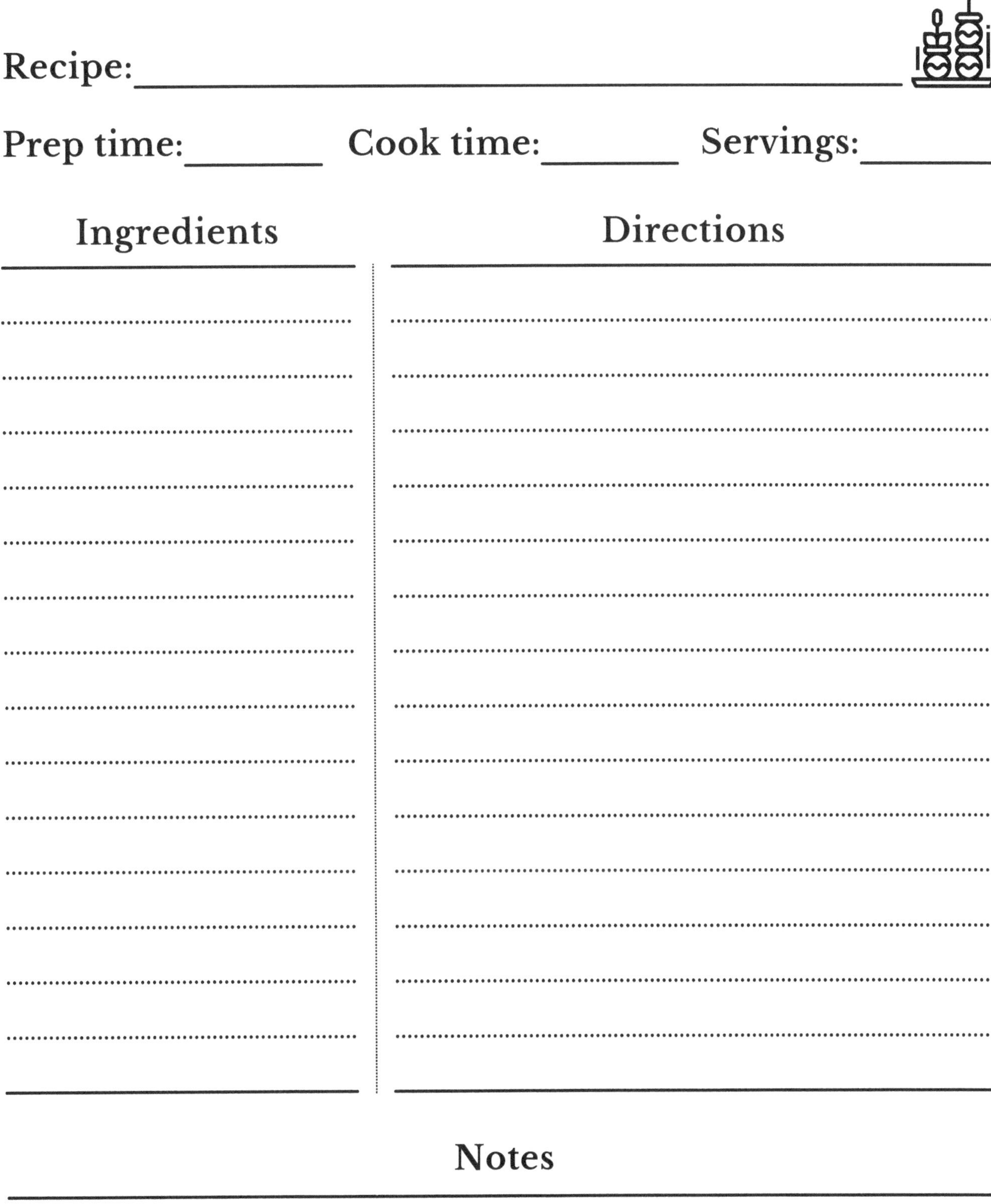

Recipe:_______________________________________

Prep time:________   Cook time:________   Servings:________

Ingredients

Directions

Notes

Recipe:____ 

Prep time:_______ Cook time:_______ Servings:_______

Ingredients | ## Directions

Notes

Recipe:_______________________________________ 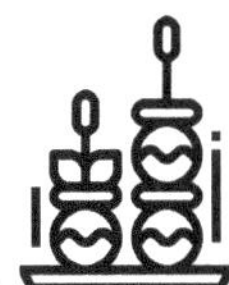

Prep time:________   Cook time:________   Servings:________

Ingredients

Directions

Notes

Recipe:_______________________________________

Prep time:________ Cook time:________ Servings:________

Ingredients	Directions

Notes

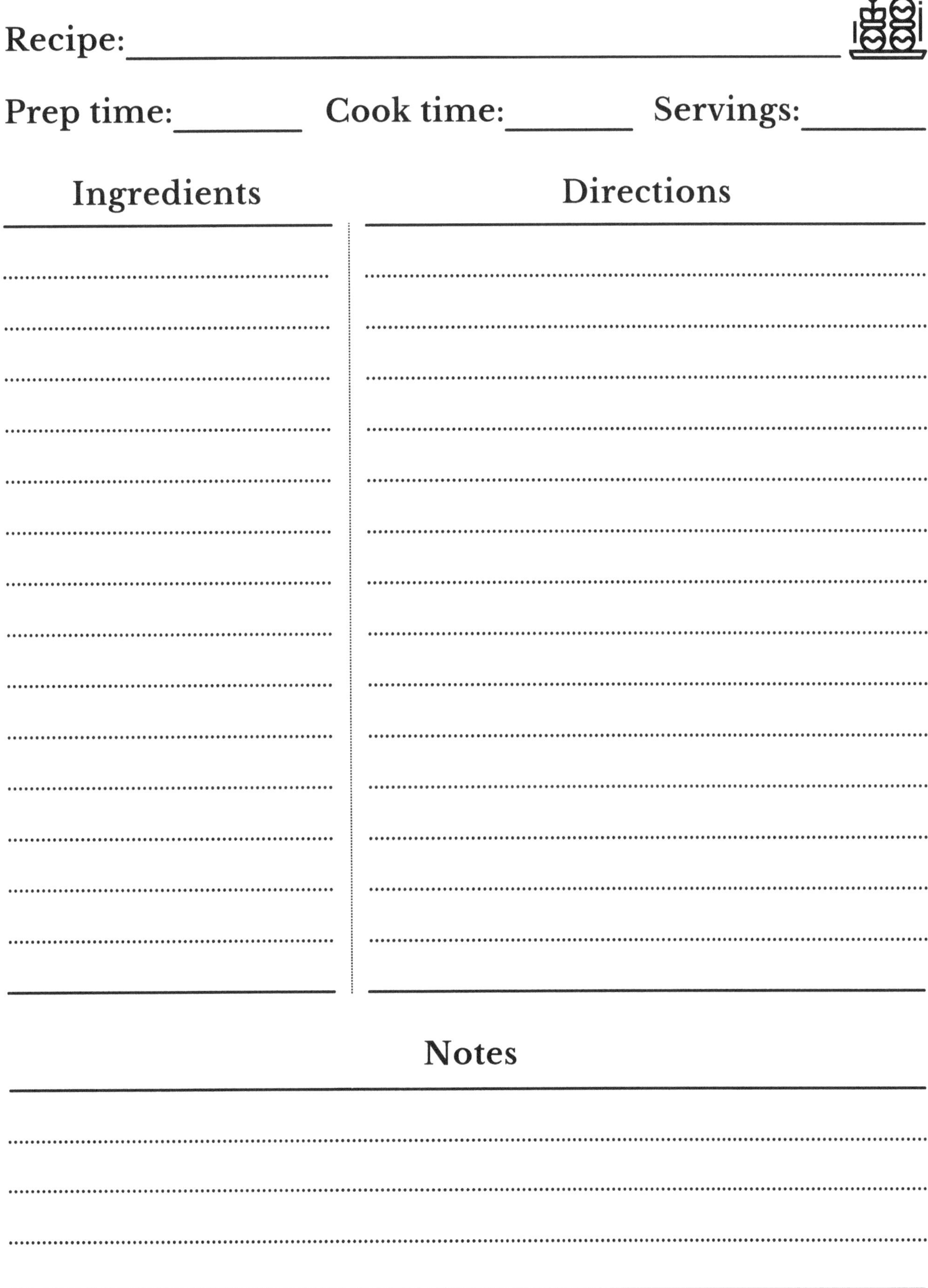

Recipe:____

Prep time:_______ Cook time:_______ Servings:_______

Ingredients

Directions

Notes

Recipe:_______________________________

Prep time:______ **Cook time:**______ **Servings:**______

Ingredients

Directions

Notes

Recipe:____ 

Prep time:_______ Cook time:_______ Servings:_______

Ingredients

Directions

Notes

Recipe:_______________________________________

Prep time:_______   Cook time:_______   Servings:_______

Ingredients

Directions

Notes

Recipe:____ 

Prep time:_______   Cook time:_______   Servings:_______

Ingredients

Directions

Notes

Recipe:

Prep time: _______ Cook time: _______ Servings: _______

Ingredients | Directions

Notes

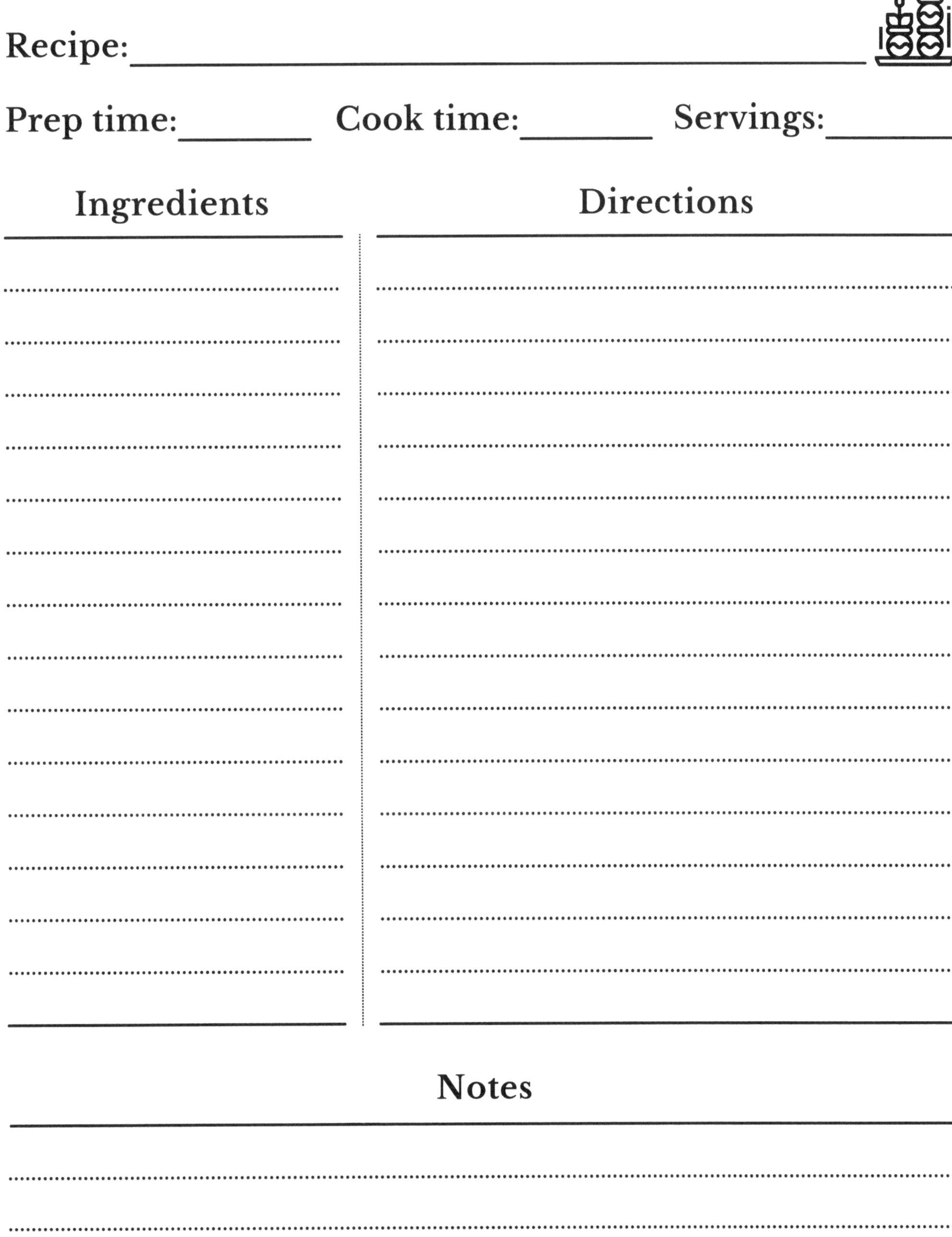

Recipe:____

Prep time:________ Cook time:________ Servings:________

Ingredients

Directions

Notes

Recipe:

Prep time:______ Cook time:______ Servings:______

Ingredients

Directions

Notes

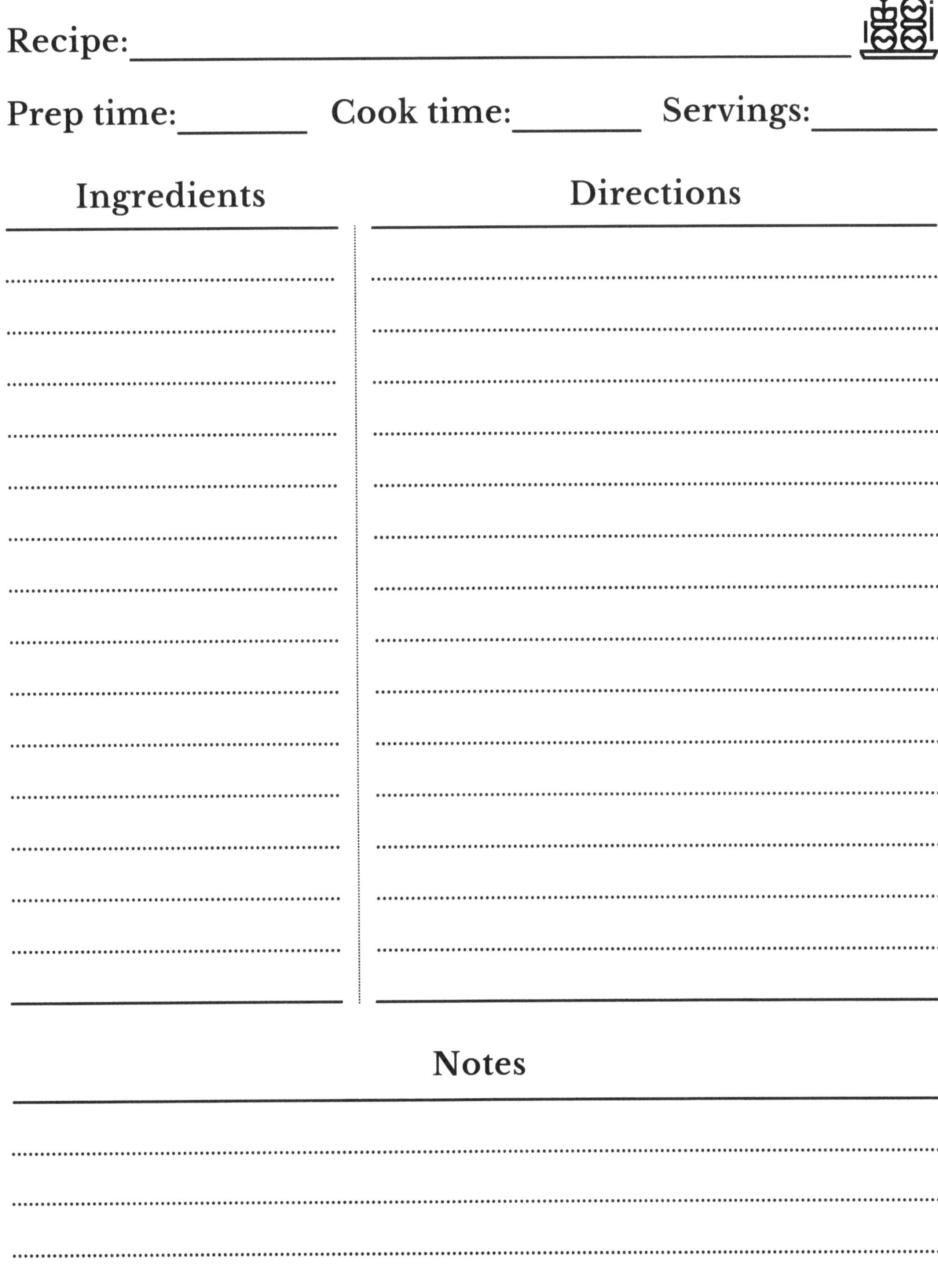

Recipe:____

Prep time:________   Cook time:________   Servings:________

Ingredients

Directions

Notes

Recipe:

Prep time:_______ Cook time:_______ Servings:_______

Ingredients

Directions

Notes

Recipe:_______________________________ 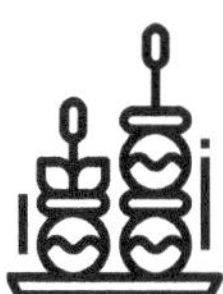

Prep time:______   Cook time:______   Servings:______

Ingredients	Directions

Notes

Recipe:____ 

Prep time:________   Cook time:________   Servings:________

Ingredients	Directions

Notes

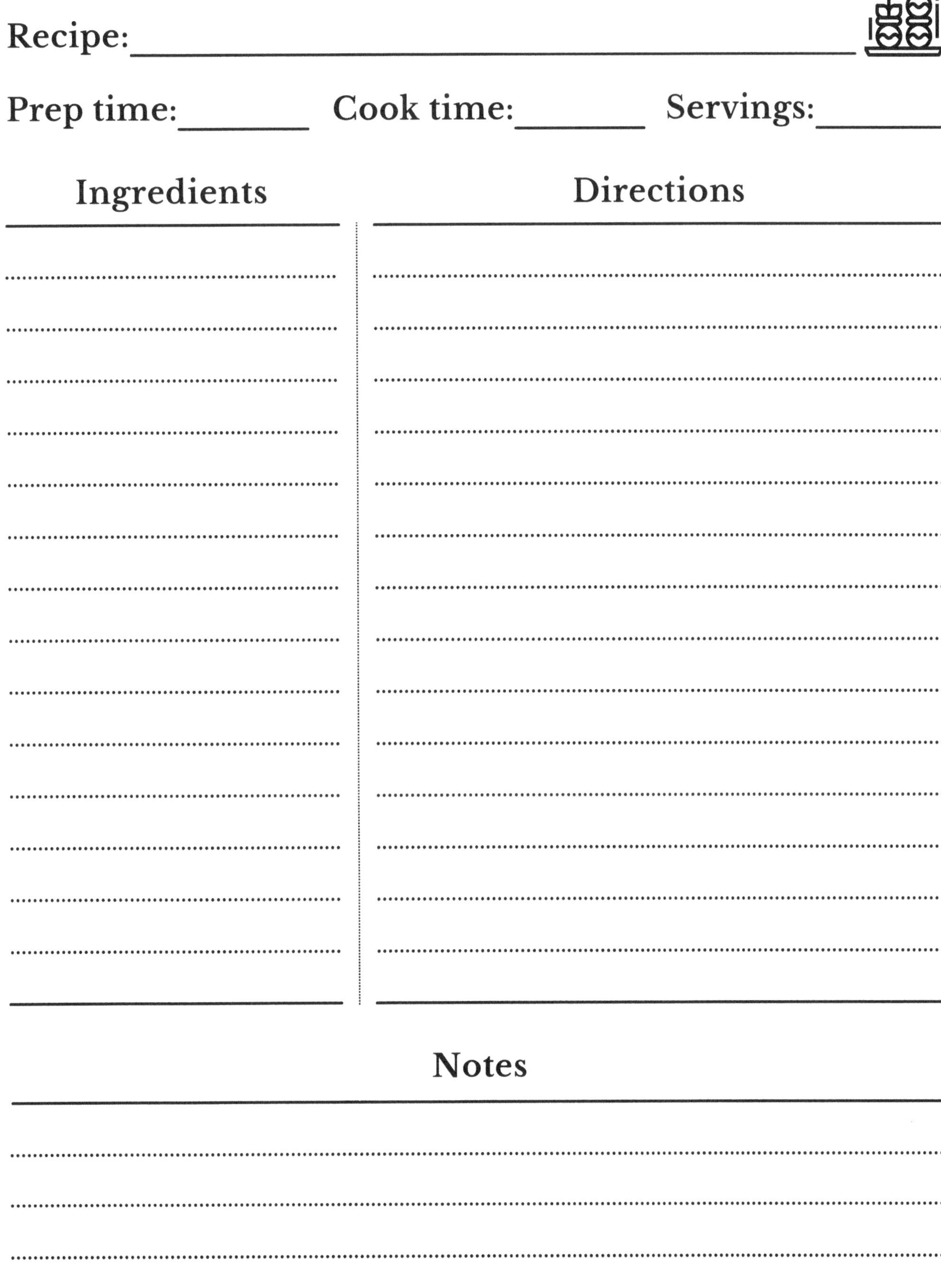

Recipe:_______________________________________

Prep time:______ Cook time:______ Servings:______

Ingredients

Directions

Notes

Recipe:_______________________ 

Prep time:________   Cook time:________   Servings:________

Ingredients	Directions

Notes

Recipe:_______________________________________ 

Prep time:_______   Cook time:_______   Servings:_______

Ingredients

Directions

Notes

Recipe:____ 

Prep time:_______ Cook time:_______ Servings:_______

Ingredients

Directions

Notes

Recipe:____ 

Prep time:________   Cook time:________   Servings:________

Ingredients	Directions

Notes

Recipe:_______________________ 

Prep time:________ **Cook time:**________ **Servings:**________

Ingredients	Directions

Notes

Recipe:_______________________________________ 

Prep time:_______   Cook time:_______   Servings:_______

Ingredients	Directions

Notes

Recipe:_______________________________________ 

Prep time:________   Cook time:________   Servings:________

Ingredients

Directions

Notes

Recipe:____ 

Prep time:________   Cook time:________   Servings:________

Ingredients

Directions

Notes

Recipe:

Prep time: ______ Cook time: ______ Servings: ______

Ingredients

Directions

Notes

Recipe:____ 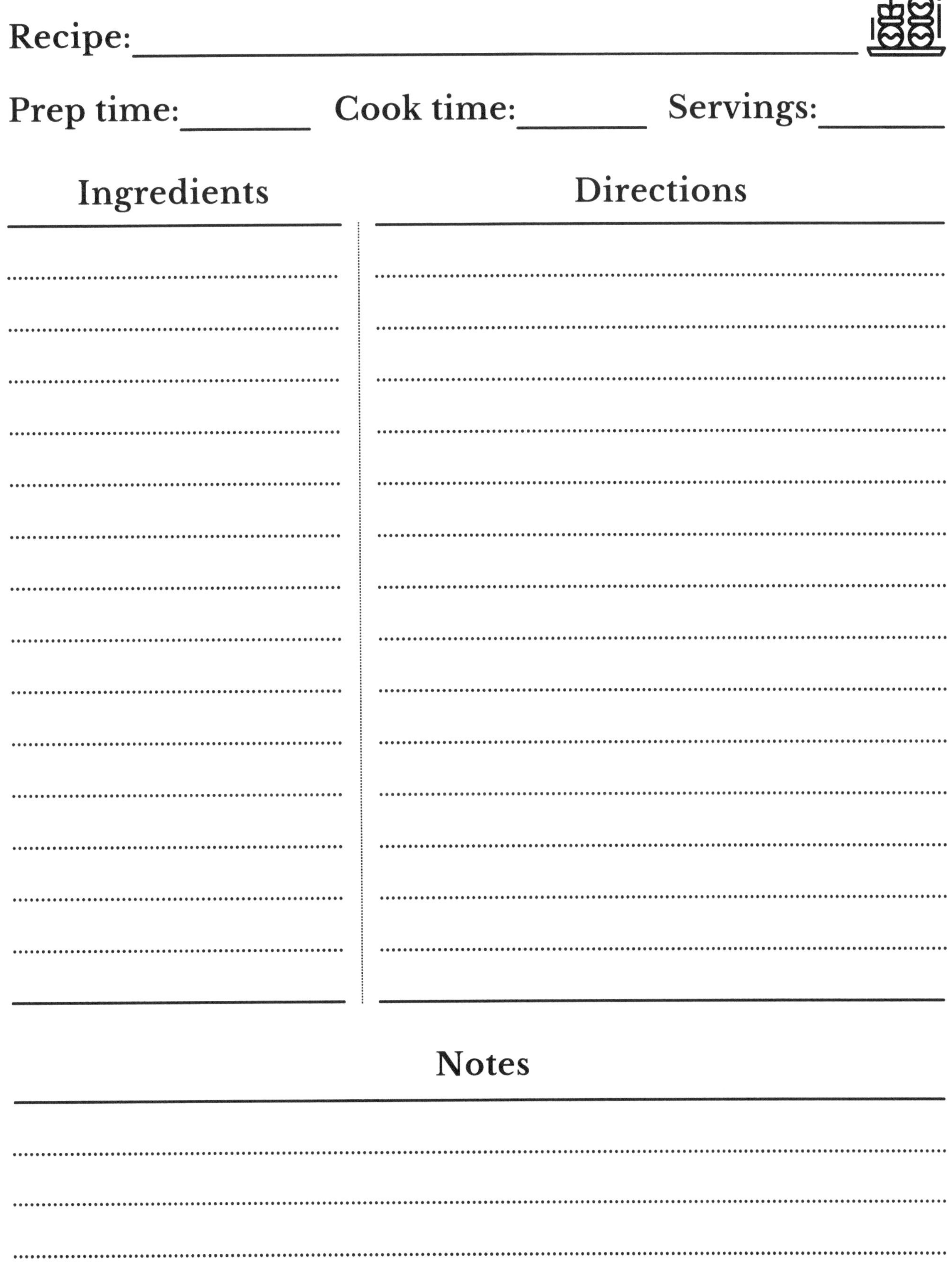

Prep time:_______   Cook time:_______   Servings:_______

Ingredients	Directions

Notes

Recipe:________________________________ 

Prep time:______ **Cook time:**______ **Servings:**______

Ingredients | Directions

Notes

Recipe:_______________________________________ 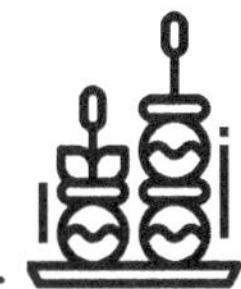

Prep time:______   Cook time:______   Servings:______

Ingredients	Directions

Notes

Recipe:

Prep time: _______ Cook time: _______ Servings: _______

Ingredients

Directions

Notes

Recipe:____ 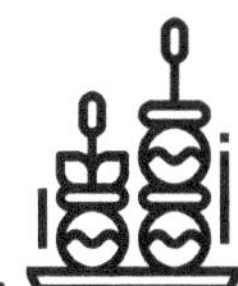

Prep time:______   Cook time:______   Servings:______

Ingredients

Directions

Notes

Recipe:____ 

Prep time:________ Cook time:________ Servings:________

Ingredients

Directions

Notes

Recipe:_______________________________________ 

Prep time:_______   Cook time:_______   Servings:_______

Ingredients

Directions

Notes

Recipe:

Prep time:_______ Cook time:_______ Servings:_______

Ingredients

Directions

Notes

Recipe:____ 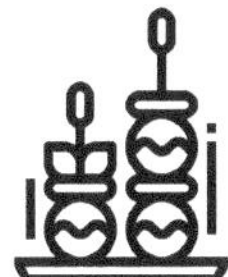

Prep time:________   Cook time:________   Servings:________

Ingredients

Directions

Notes

Recipe:_______________________________________ 

Prep time:________ Cook time:________ Servings:________

Ingredients

Directions

Notes

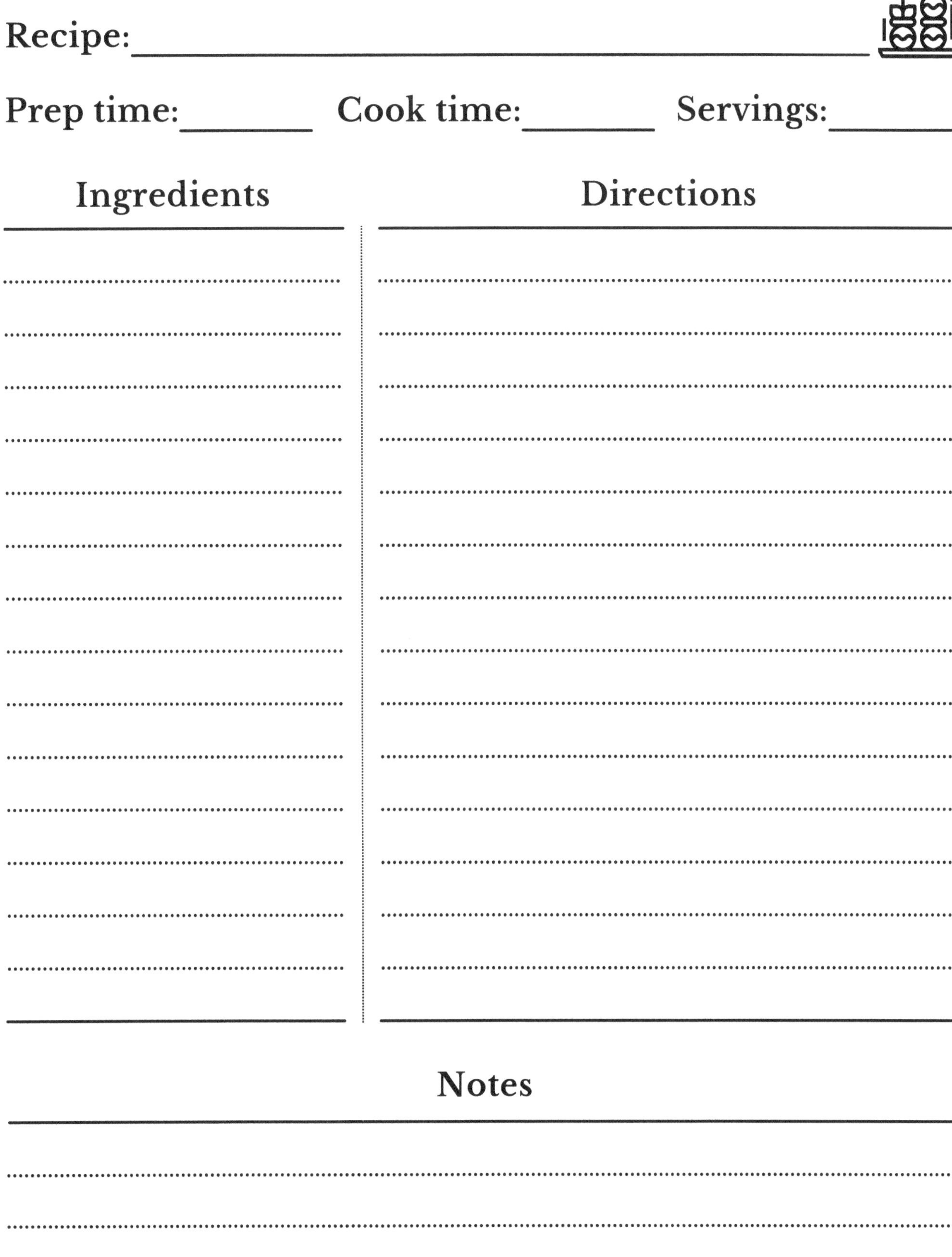

Recipe:____

Prep time:________   Cook time:________   Servings:________

Ingredients	Directions

Notes

Recipe:____ 

Prep time:_______   Cook time:_______   Servings:_______

Ingredients

Directions

Notes

Recipe:

Prep time: ______ Cook time: ______ Servings: ______

Ingredients

Directions

Notes

Recipe: _______________________________

Prep time: _______ Cook time: _______ Servings: _______

Ingredients

Directions

Notes

Recipe:_______________________________________ 

Prep time:________   Cook time:________   Servings:________

Ingredients

Directions

Notes

Recipe:_______________________________________

Prep time:________ Cook time:________ Servings:________

Ingredients

Directions

Notes

Recipe:____ 

Prep time:________   Cook time:________   Servings:________

Ingredients	Directions

Notes

Recipe:

Prep time:_______ Cook time:_______ Servings:_______

Ingredients

Directions

Notes

Recipe:_______________________ 

Prep time:______ **Cook time:**______ **Servings:**______

Ingredients

Directions

Notes

Recipe:

Prep time:_______ Cook time:_______ Servings:_______

Ingredients

Directions

Notes

Recipe: _______________________________

Prep time: _______   Cook time: _______   Servings: _______

Ingredients

Directions

Notes

Recipe:_______________________________________

Prep time:________ Cook time:________ Servings:________

Ingredients

Directions

Notes

Recipe:

Prep time: _______ **Cook time:** _______ **Servings:** _______

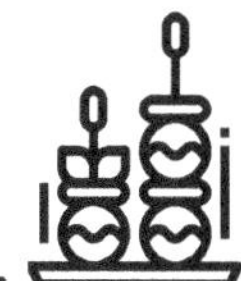

Ingredients

Directions

Notes

Recipe:

Prep time:_______ **Cook time:**_______ **Servings:**_______

Ingredients

Directions

Notes

Recipe:_______________________________________ 

Prep time:_______   Cook time:_______   Servings:_______

Ingredients	Directions

Notes

Recipe:

Prep time: _______ **Cook time:** _______ **Servings:** _______

Ingredients

Directions

Notes

Recipe:____ 

Prep time:________   Cook time:________   Servings:________

Ingredients

Directions

Notes

Recipe:_______________________________________ 

Prep time:________ **Cook time:**________ **Servings:**________

Ingredients

Directions

Notes

Recipe:_______________________________________ 

Prep time:_______   Cook time:_______   Servings:_______

Ingredients	Directions

Notes

Recipe:_______________________________________ 

Prep time:________ Cook time:________ Servings:________

Ingredients

Directions

Notes

Recipe:

Prep time: _______ Cook time: _______ Servings: _______

Ingredients

Directions

Notes

Recipe:

Prep time:_______ **Cook time:**_______ **Servings:**_______ 

Ingredients

Directions

Notes

Recipe:____ 

Prep time:_________   Cook time:_________   Servings:_________

Ingredients

Directions

Notes

Recipe:____ 

Prep time:______ Cook time:______ Servings:______

Ingredients

Directions

Notes

Recipe:____ 

Prep time:_______   Cook time:_______   Servings:_______

Ingredients

Directions

Notes

Recipe:____ 

Prep time:________ Cook time:________ Servings:________

Ingredients

Directions

Notes

Recipe:

Prep time:________ Cook time:________ Servings:________

Ingredients	Directions

Notes

Recipe:

Prep time: ________ **Cook time:** ________ **Servings:** ________

Ingredients

Directions

Notes

Recipe:____ 

Prep time:________   Cook time:________   Servings:________

Ingredients	Directions

Notes

Recipe:____ 

Prep time:_______ Cook time:_______ Servings:_______

Ingredients

Directions

Notes

Recipe: _______________________________________ 

Prep time: _______   Cook time: _______   Servings: _______

Ingredients	Directions

Notes

Recipe:

Prep time:_______ Cook time:_______ Servings:_______

Ingredients

Directions

Notes

Recipe:____ 

Prep time:_______   Cook time:_______   Servings:_______

Ingredients

Directions

....

....

....

....

....

....

....

....

....

....

....

....

Notes

....

....

....

Recipe:

Prep time: _______   Cook time: _______   Servings: _______

Ingredients

Directions

Notes

Recipe:______________________________________ 

Prep time:______   Cook time:______   Servings:______

Ingredients

Directions

Notes

Recipe:

Prep time: ______ **Cook time:** ______ **Servings:** ______

Ingredients

Directions

Notes

Recipe:_______________________________ 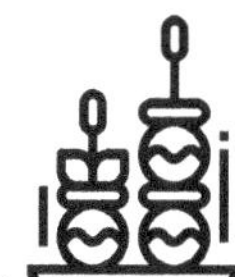

Prep time:______ Cook time:______ Servings:______

Ingredients	Directions

Notes

Recipe:_______________________________________ 

Prep time:________   Cook time:________   Servings:________

Ingredients	Directions

Notes

Recipe: ____

Prep time: _______ Cook time: _______ Servings: _______

Ingredients

Directions

Notes

Recipe:____ 

Prep time:________ Cook time:________ Servings:________

Ingredients

Directions

Notes

Recipe:_______________________________ 

Prep time:_______   Cook time:_______   Servings:_______

Ingredients

Directions

Notes

Recipe:______________________________ 

Prep time:_______ Cook time:_______ Servings:_______

Ingredients

Directions

Notes

Recipe:____ 

Prep time:________ Cook time:________ Servings:________

Ingredients

Directions

Notes

Recipe:____ 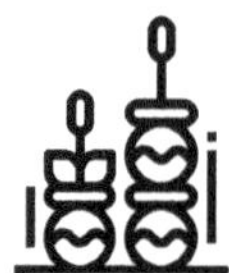

Prep time:________ Cook time:________ Servings:________

Ingredients

Directions

Notes

Recipe:

Prep time: _______ **Cook time:** _______ **Servings:** _______

Ingredients

Directions

Notes

Recipe:_______________________________________ 

Prep time:________ Cook time:________ Servings:________

Ingredients

Directions

Notes

Recipe:

Prep time:______ **Cook time:**______ **Servings:**______

Ingredients

Directions

Notes

Recipe:

Prep time: _______ Cook time: _______ Servings: _______

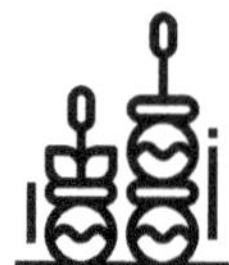

Ingredients

Directions

Notes

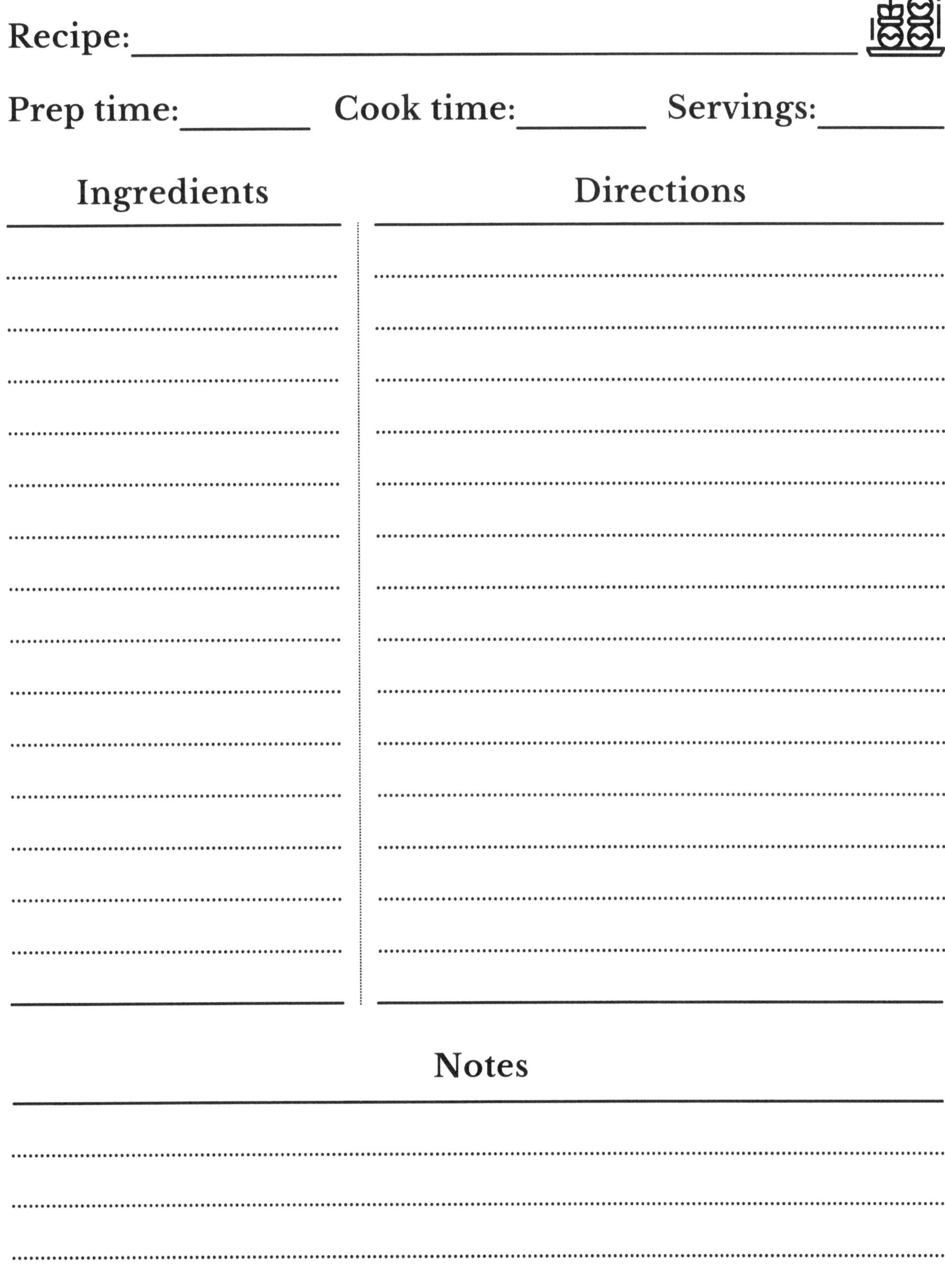

Recipe:____

Prep time:________ Cook time:________ Servings:________

Ingredients

Directions

Notes

Recipe: _______________________________________

Prep time: _______ **Cook time:** _______ **Servings:** _______

Ingredients

Directions

Notes

Recipe: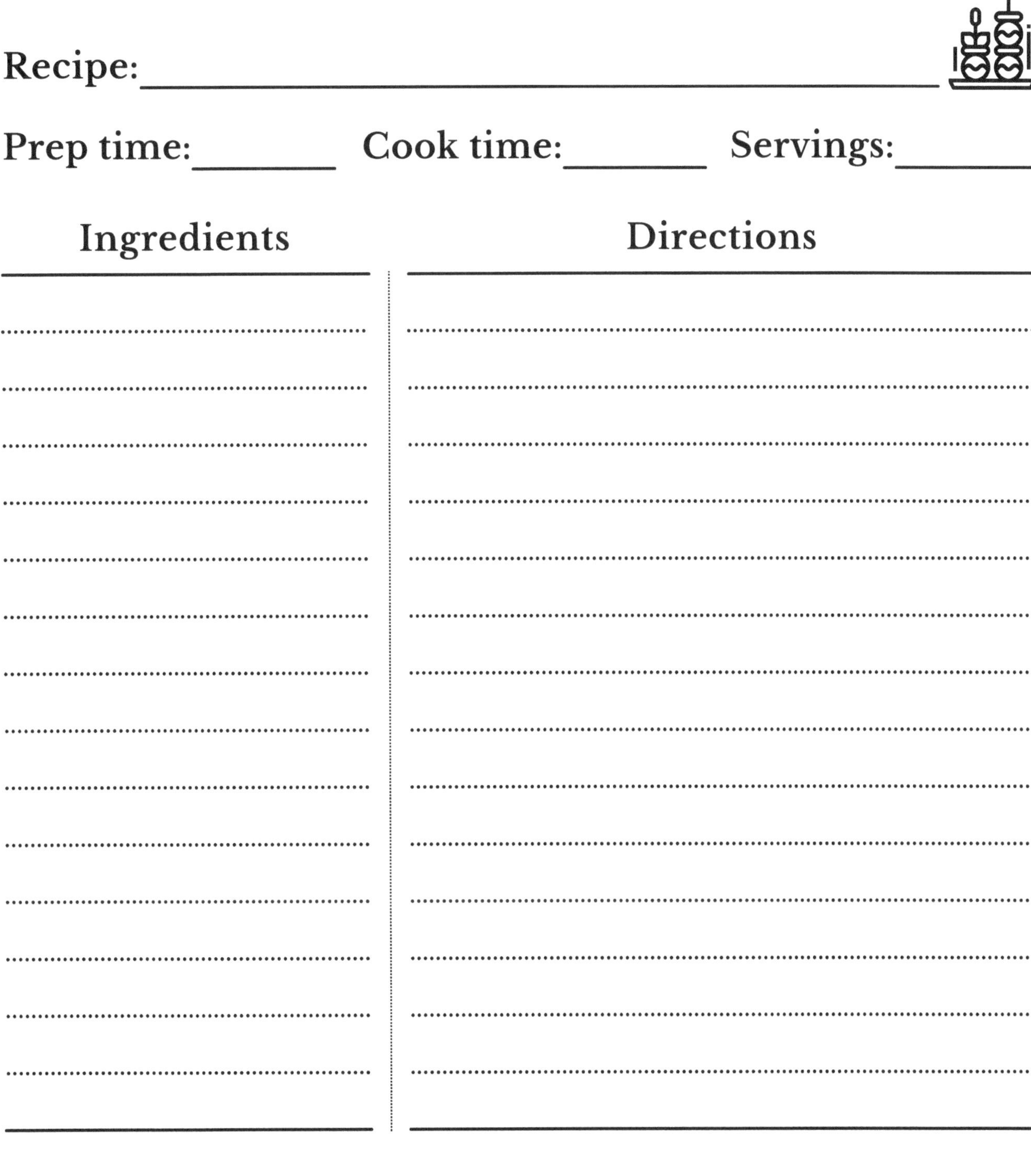

Prep time:_______   Cook time:_______   Servings:_______

Ingredients   Directions

Notes

Recipe:____ 

Prep time:________ Cook time:________ Servings:________

Ingredients

Directions

Notes

Recipe:____ 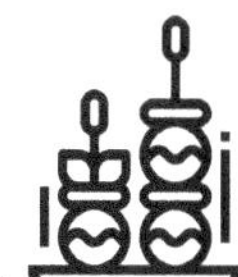

Prep time:________   Cook time:________   Servings:________

Ingredients	Directions

Notes

Recipe:

Prep time: ________ **Cook time:** ________ **Servings:** ________

Ingredients

Directions

Notes